Advice My Parents Gave Me

and Other Lessons I Learned From My Mistakes

Rodolfo Costa

Copyright © 2009 Rodolfo Costa.

All rights reserved.

www.advicemyparentsgaveme.com

Admypagame Series

No part of this book may be reproduced in any form or stored in a retrieval system or transmitted by any means without the written permission of the author.

ISBN: 10:1466311053
ISBN-13:978-1466311053

2011 Revised edition

A collection of 409 thoughts, quotes, lessons, ideas, suggestions, reminders, words of advice and encouragement to lead a successful, rewarding, peaceful, happy, and fulfilling life.

Thanks to my parents, who tried hard to instill in me some of the lessons, advice, and ideas you are about to read, to my son, Marco, who helped me realize how much patience I have, to my brother, sisters, and to my friends, for all their support and encouragement. I am thankful for my life and the problems and setbacks that have helped me build character, grow, and evolve as a person and human being. Thanks to all the readers of this book—I wish you the best.

CONTENTS

Introduction.. 1

1. Positive Attitude and Optimism........................ 13
2. Responsibility and Inspiration......................... 21
3. Goals and Motivation................................... 29
4. Action, Persistence and Success....................... 37
5. Self-Doubt, Fear and Criticism........................ 47
6. Positive Thinking and Communication.............. 55
7. Positive Self-Esteem and Good Manners............ 63
8. Learning and Understanding........................... 71
9. Money.. 79
10. Planning, Past, Present and Future................... 85
11. Laughing and Taking it Easy.......................... 91
12. Love and Relationships................................. 97
13. Children... 105
14. Forgiveness and Acceptance.......................... 109
15. Happiness and Awareness............................. 115
16. Gratitude and Getting Older.......................... 125

Final Thoughts 131

About the Author... 135

INTRODUCTION

This book is a collection of 409 thoughts, quotes, lessons, ideas, suggestions, reminders, words of advice and encouragement about life in general that were passed on to me by my parents or that I learned at one time or another throughout my life. It includes lessons I have learned from my mistakes and from my share of problems and setbacks. It touches on attitude, goals, responsibility, persistence, success, relationships, planning, personal/spiritual growth, and fulfillment.

This book is about seeing and experiencing life in a different way, about growing and evolving as a person and human being. You may already know, or may have heard, some of the advice, ideas, and lessons you are about to read. I hope and wish you are already implementing them in your life, but if not, perhaps you just need a little reminding—we all do. You may be reading some of the lessons for the first time. You may not agree with some of them. That is fine—we do not always share the same opinions and ideas—but I hope this book inspires you to think and reflect about your own life, your dreams, your goals, your aspirations, your circumstances, and your relationships. I want you to build the courage to create your own ideas, and to live your life to the fullest, striving to reach all of your dreams and goals, whatever they may be, so you can become a better, and more fulfilled, person than you were before. I want you to enjoy your family, your friends, and your time alone, to "slow down to smell the roses" and enjoy your life in general.

This book is about giving yourself choices without getting consumed with daily life. Do not ignore your daily responsibilities, but do not get consumed by them. Plan for tomorrow but live for today—live in the "now." If you do what you need to do today, to the best of your ability, to accomplish your dreams and to live the life you want, tomorrow will take care of itself. Since all you have is today, squeeze every single minute of it and begin your change *now*.

I had been thinking about writing this book for a long time as I was hearing my parents' voices in my mind and reliving some of the advice and life lessons I am about to share with you. But I just never got around to it. There was always some excuse, some interference—something more "important." Time seemed to be moving faster and faster in front of my eyes, but I did not want to notice. I finally stopped giving myself excuses not to do it and set up a deadline—my fiftieth birthday.

Like most of us, I have had my share of successes and disappointments, but I must say that, overall, life has been wonderful to me. Unfortunately, for a while I was too busy within my own world to realize that and became complacent. Now, after doing some soul searching, thinking about my life experiences, my ups and downs, my joys and sorrows, my dreams and plans, my achievements and disappointments—my existence in general—I can say with all conviction that I am grateful for what I have learned from my parents, grateful for what I have experienced, grateful for what I have been taught by every one of life's battles, especially the ones that I lost. I am grateful for my existence. This is how I choose to think, and now this is how I choose my life to be—*wonderful!* No excuses!

Unfortunately, most of us live by default. We all have dreams, ideas, and plans for our lives, for what we want to achieve, for what we want to become, yet a lot of us never accomplish what we dream. For one reason or another, we do not really seem to want what we say we want— although we say we want it—we lack the motivation, enthusiasm, and determination to get it. This may be because we do not see or have an idea as to how we are going to turn our dreams into reality, so we never give ourselves the opportunities to make them happen.

I always heard "dream until your dreams come true," but I also learned that dreaming alone would not make those dreams come true; I had to take some action to realize and fulfill them.

Many of us see our lives pass in front of our eyes while we are worrying and waiting for all the pieces of the puzzle to be ready and perfect before we can move ahead. We are waiting for the right time to act, and the right time never seems to come; we make excuses to make ourselves feel better about our lack of motivation and determination, and perhaps to make peace with our egos and self-esteem.

We tell everybody why we did not do and accomplish what we wanted to do, why we are where we are. We are looking for validation from others. Perhaps, we want them to tell us that yes, indeed, it is not our fault, that is how life is; there is nothing we can do. But in truth, if you want things to change in your life, if you want to make your dreams come true, you are the only one who can do it no matter what your present circumstances are.

Do not wait any longer. Take charge of your life. Set your mind to start now. Forget about the past—it is gone. Do not worry about the future—it is not here yet. Create the desire to change your current situation and circumstances. Nobody is going to do it for you. The right time to begin is now; no more excuses! The sooner you act, the closer you will get to your dream, because time does not wait.

Stop being a victim, stop creating self-imposed limitations, and stop the excuses. Many world-class achievers have had problems or disadvantages in their lives. They were raised in poverty, have some physical disability, or were abandoned or abused when they were children. They have had many obstacles and setbacks that they overcame one way or another and they are where they are now because of their motivation and determination to triumph over their situations, without being victims, without giving up, and without surrendering to their circumstances.

You are the only one who can make the decision to change and live the life you dream. Life is about choices; every day, every single situation we face involves that we make a choice. We choose how we react to life's challenges and opportunities. Some choices, of course, are easier than others, but, in essence, we choose how to live our lives.

Stop worrying about tomorrow and about things that may not happen. Most of our lives are filled with setbacks, disappointments, aches of the heart, "failures," and tragedies in general, but the funny thing is that the majority of them never actually happened. They are all in our heads—we create all the stress and worry in our lives. If you want to change, create, or start something new, you have to apply yourself and begin now. Make the decision to change and to be a more fulfilled and better person, because if you are going to wait for something to take place or all the pieces of the puzzle to be ready and perfect, nothing is ever going to happen. You will keep on waiting and waiting and then blame everybody else or the circumstances for your setbacks, shortcomings, and lack of success.

Get up and start moving forward, do it little by little, and remember—progress is what counts—not perfection. A five hundred-page book is written one word at the time; you prepare for a marathon one step at a time. The longer you wait, the further you will be from your dream, from becoming the person you always wanted to be. Decide to change *now*.

Advice My Parents Gave Me

and Other Lessons I Learned From My Mistakes

The greatest discovery of my generation is that human beings can alter their lives by altering their attitude of mind.

William James

To everyone is given the key to heaven; the same key opens the gates of hell.

Ancient Proverb

Attitude is more important than the past, than education, than money, than circumstances, than what people do or say. It is more important than appearance, giftedness, or skill.

Charles Swindoll

1

POSITIVE ATTITUDE and OPTIMISM

1. Life is wonderful, life is horrible, life is fabulous, life is terrible, life is great, life is awful, life is challenging, life is "a piece of cake", life is unfair, life is beautiful, life is ugly, life is tough, life is easy ... In reality, life is whatever you make it.

2. The way you feel is a decision that you make every day. It is sometimes a conscious decision and sometimes an unconscious one. Be more in touch with your thoughts and feelings and make the decision to start every day, in a positive and optimistic way.

3   There is a choice in every situation you face. You can see it in either a positive or a negative way. You can feel happy or you can feel miserable—the choice is always yours.

4   Your attitude is everything. Always try to maintain a positive attitude about things. This will help you build the courage to change things, it will help you find the serenity to accept things you cannot change, and it will give you the wisdom to know the difference. Gain power over your attitude.

5   Work on your attitude. Learn to control it before it controls you.

6   A positive attitude is far more important than aptitude for a successful life.

7   You cannot change a lot of things that happen in your life, but you can always change how you react to what happens in your life.

8   Do not focus and waste your energy on the "little problems" of your daily life. Do not allow yourself to make them bigger than they are.

9 Be an optimist. Learn to see and appreciate what life offers you. Concentrate on the positive and the beautiful things in your life.

10 Try to look for the good and positive in bad situations.

11 Be alert and pay attention to what is going on around you. Opportunities come in many shapes and forms—many times your setbacks or problems are opportunities in "disguise."

12 Be creative—use your imagination. Take those opportunities and turn them into successes.

13 Eliminate the word "failure" from your vocabulary and replace it with "learning experience."

14 Remember the word "failure" is just a state of mind. Approach it with a positive attitude and you will notice that it will become a learning experience toward your success.

15 There are no failures in life, only results—positive or negative. If you do not get the result you want, look for options, make

adjustments, and try a different approach until you get the result you want.

16 Always look for better ways to do things. Be proactive and be a part of a solution, not a part of a problem.

17 Use your wisdom and common sense to create positive changes in your life.

18 You are not finished when you do not get the result you want, you are finished when you give up. Never give up!

19 Trust your intuition. Have faith, confidence, and belief in yourself. You are capable of creating and achieving great and wonderful things in your life.

20 You are the one who creates your life, and you are the one who creates your future.

21 Be in charge of your destiny. If you do not control your future, somebody else will.

22 Allow yourself to see beyond what others think is possible, wise, or practical. You can create a different reality and make a

different life for yourself. In the end, your success will be more rewarding.

23 Your purpose in life is whatever you choose and want it to be. It is up to you to decide.

24 There is no limit to what you can achieve. Determine how far you want to go and develop the necessary strength to help you get there.

25 Enlighten yourself and discover what you are capable of. Aim high—aim for the stars.

26 Cultivate an optimistic mind, use your imagination, always consider alternatives, and dare to believe that you can make possible what others think is impossible.

There are two primary choices in life: to accept conditions as they exist, or accept the responsibility for changing them.

Denis Waitley

In the long run, we shape our lives, and we shape ourselves. The process never ends until we die. And the choices we make are ultimately our own responsibility.

Eleanor Roosevelt

Life is a gift, and it offers us the privilege, opportunity, and responsibility to give something back by becoming more.

Tony Robbins

Man must cease attributing his problems to his environment, and learn again to exercise his will - his personal responsibility in the realm of faith and morals.

Albert Schweitzer

Your present circumstances don't determine where you can go; they merely determine where you start.

Nido Qubein

2

RESPONSIBILITY and INSPIRATION

27 Take responsibility for your actions and consequences.

28 Take responsibility for your own life and circumstances.

29 Always keep your promises and honor you commitments. Give your word and carry it through—even if it is difficult, expensive or inconvenient.

30 Be accountable and you will get the respect and trust of others.

31 Remember that people may doubt your words, but they will always believe your actions.

32 Be honest, loyal, and fair even if it is not to your advantage. Never compromise your personal integrity.

33 Acknowledge and recognize your mistakes. Learn from them and move on and try not to repeat them. Do not beat yourself up in the process. Nobody is perfect; we are only human.

34 If you made a mistake or did something wrong, set your ego aside. Apologize with sincerity and mean it. People will appreciate that, and they will not feel used or taken for granted.

35 Stop whining, complaining, and blaming others for your mistakes, problems, misfortunes, and setbacks. That kind of negative behavior is not going to get you any closer to where you want to go. It will only make you bitter and frustrated.

36 Try to do what you must do, even though you think it is difficult. If you never try, it will always be difficult.

37 Take a good and careful look at your situation. Decide what you really want to accomplish, build the enthusiasm, and go for it.

38 Do not become a victim and feel sorry for yourself. Do not expect people to feel sorry for you. If you fall, get up, dust yourself off, and try again.

39 Do not give in to adversity—do not give up hope. Understand that adversity could be the best teacher you ever had.

40 Visualize yourself as the person you want to be, act like the person you want to be, and strive to become the person you want to become.

41 Allow yourself some time to think. See where you are now and make the

commitment to change your life by going after your dreams.

42 We all encounter problems at one point or another in our lives. Deal with them to the best of your ability without whining and complaining.

43 Accept and face your problems. Understand that they are part of life. They are teachers of valuable lessons, and they are the opportunities for your personal growth.

44 You may be confronted with a problem that seems to have no solution and you may feel as if there is nowhere to go. Go ahead, take a break, but do not quit. Have faith. Let your mind and body rest, ask for guidance, and come back later with more energy and motivation.

45 Things change—circumstances change. Learn to adapt. Adjust your efforts and yourself to what is presented to you so you can respond accordingly.

46 Never see change as a threat—do not get intimidated by it. Change can be an

opportunity to learn, to grow, to evolve, and to become a better person.

47 Sometimes what you may see as the end could be the start of a new and better beginning.

48 Be wise. Make the commitment to change the direction of your life if you do not like where you are going.

49 You have to wake up if you want your dreams to come true.

50 The world belongs to those who have the courage to create the possibility of realizing their dreams.

51 Keep active and think about everything—all the time. Inspiration comes with action and stray thoughts often lead to great ideas and solutions.

52 Live every day as if it were your last. Create the desire and build the passion to take advantage of every minute—we only live once and time does not wait for anybody.

If you don't know where you are going, you will probably end up somewhere else.

Lawrence J. Peter

Obstacles are those frightful things you see when you take your eyes off your goal.

Henry Ford

Your goals are the road maps that guide you and show you what is possible for your life.

Les Brown

If you aim at nothing, you'll hit it every time.

Unknown

A year from now you may wish you had started today.

Karen Lamb

Some of the world's greatest feats were accomplished by people not smart enough to know they were impossible.

Doug Larson

3
GOALS and MOTIVATION

53 Face your reality with courage. Realize that you have the ability and the potential to alter your future in a positive way.

54 Have goals. Goals make you focus on what it is that you want to achieve.

55 Goals give you a purpose, a sense of direction. They add meaning to your life.

56 Give yourself a target, prepare a plan and go for your goal. You will never hit your target if you do not have one.

57 Establish goals for yourself, no matter how big, crazy, or unattainable they may seem. Who are you not to achieve them and be

successful? Who are you not to be the person you want to be? Believe in yourself.

58 Write your goals down. Set in writing your immediate, intermediate, and final goals. Go over your list and read them aloud daily. Let your subconscious mind know what you want.

59 After writing down your goals, make specific plans to achieve them. Work at those goals every day.

60 Start now building the motivation to make your goals a reality. Stop waiting for everything to be perfect before you begin.

61 Do not be overwhelmed with or intimidated by the unknown. As you work to make your goals a reality, you will notice that all of the pieces of the puzzle will start fitting and falling into place, and everything will start to make more sense.

62 The desire to reach your goals must be stronger than the fear you may have of not accomplishing them.

63 Every time you achieve your goals, you grow and become more confident in your abilities to make your other dreams come true.

64 Follow your dreams until their realization. Do and learn as you go. Progress will guide you. Progress is what counts, not perfection.

65 If your goal seems overwhelming, set smaller goals that will help you get closer to your big goal. Set timelines to accomplish them and continue one step at a time.

66 You will discover that when you have long-term goals, you will not be bothered, frustrated, or discouraged by short-term difficulties and setbacks.

67 Focus on your vision and take action to make your dreams a reality—keep on dreaming until your dreams come true.

68 Commit yourself to what you want to achieve, to what you want to create, to what you want to become. When you commit yourself to achieving your goals and dreams many forces in the universe begin to work

in your favor. These forces make possible the creation and realization of great and wonderful things in your life that we sometimes call coincidences.

69 Do not get overwhelmed with too many details— just keep your eyes on your goal.

70 Many people who accomplished great things did not know how they were going to accomplish them. They had a goal and everything else were just "details."

71 Use your imagination to design what you want to bring to reality. Imagine and feel what you want to accomplish, what you want to create, and commit yourself to doing it. Do not just fantasize.

72 There is one goal that you cannot achieve— the one that you do not try to achieve.

73 Believe with all your heart that you can reach your goals. Something is only impossible until someone proves it otherwise.

74 Have faith in yourself and visualize the outcome. Make a habit of drawing detailed

pictures of the goal you want to achieve. Create the feeling as if you have already achieved it.

75 Employ your emotions and all of your senses to visualize the achievement of your goal. Imagine the way it feels, smells, sounds, and tastes.

76 The combination of imagination, visualization, and action is more important than knowledge.

77 What you imagine *inside* of you will help you bring to reality what you will create and manifest *outside* of you.

78 Act with the drive, the will, the passion, and the desire necessary to realize your goals.

79 It is OK to be down occasionally—we all have those moments—but it is not OK to stay down.

80 Always concentrate on the path that you have planned for yourself. Strive to be the best that you can be. Dare to be great!

Do you want to know who you are? Don't ask. Act! Action will delineate and define you.

Thomas Jefferson

There is no better time than now. The time to live is now. The time to dream is now. The time to imagine and forget the past is now. The time to shine is now. The time to bleed, sweat, and determine yourself for the things you want most is now.

Unknown

Patience and perseverance have a magical effect before which difficulties disappear and obstacles vanish.

John Quincy Adams

The best way to get something done is to begin.

Unknown

I've missed over nine thousand shots in my career. I've lost almost three hundred games. Twenty-six times, I've been trusted to take the game-winning shot ... and missed. I've failed over and over and over again in my life. And that is why I succeed.

Michael Jordan

4

ACTION, PERSISTENCE and SUCCESS

81 Do not wait—begin now. Your task may appear to be hard today but it will become easy later on if you persevere.

82 Act now! Take advantage of every day, every hour, and every minute to do what you need to do to create or correct a situation. If you do not act, you will never know how much you can achieve.

83 Do not leave for tomorrow what you can do today. Do it now. You do not know what tomorrow will bring. Even though you may have a perfect plan of action, tomorrow is still a question mark.

84 Do not wait for all the conditions to be perfect before you act, or you will never act. Get things done. Deal with problems as they arise.

85 Practice self-discipline. Learn to make yourself do the things you have to do when they ought to be done, whether you feel like it or not.

86 Motivate yourself often and create the spark to bring to your life what you want. Find the strength to keep yourself moving forward when things are not working as you had planned.

87 Do not be impatient—good things come to those who wait. Just do what you need to do when you need to do it—do not despair—success may be just around the corner.

88 Be persistent in building the foundation that will support your success—do not stop.

89 Do not sit still; start moving now. In the beginning, you may not go in the direction you want, but as long as you are moving,

you are creating alternatives and possibilities.

90 Put the law of averages to work in your favor—the more times and things you try—the closer you will get to your success.

91 It may take little time to get where you want to be, but if you pause and think for a moment, you will notice that you are no longer where you were. Do not stop—keep going.

92 Do not fool yourself into thinking that you will get your rewards right away. Do not look for instant gratification. You always get the prize at the end of the race, not at the beginning—every step you take forward will get you closer to the finish line, to the prize that you want.

93 Do not procrastinate—recognize the fear that you may feel when attempting to move forward, but go ahead and do it anyway. Your future depends on you.

94 Work on your desires and make them a reality. Your success is determined by your

ability to reach your goals in life, whatever they may be.

95 Do not quit. Do not give up. Your dream may be closer than you think, but if you are not willing to take another step, and another, and another, you may never see it and you may never know how close you were to achieving it.

96 Try to do much better today than you did yesterday. Each day, try to accomplish more than you did the day before. Push yourself and strive to achieve your dreams to the best of your abilities.

97 Many of us see things and say, "Why?" Instead, expand your curiosity, imagination, creativity, and desire and ask yourself, "Why not?"

98 Keep moving forward. Be willing to do the little things that you can do without being too concerned about the big things that you cannot do. Otherwise, you will end up doing nothing.

99 Do not get so caught up trying to achieve success to the point that you lose sight of the

real essence of your life—Success is a journey, not a destination.

100 Remember that most of us have the talent to succeed in life, but not many are willing to take the time and effort to succeed, because it involves commitment, discipline, persistence, sacrifice, and work.

101 Success is not a straight line. You will have to adjust all the time in order to get to your correct destination.

102 Success is a choice and it has a different meaning for each one of us, but whatever your meaning of success is, never give up until you are successful.

103 Successful people do what unsuccessful people will not. Strive to be among the successful people.

104 Develop the passion, the willpower, and the drive to succeed. Be passionate about what you want to accomplish and do whatever it is that you need to do in order to bring your dream to a reality.

105 Success does not depend on how much you know, whom you know, how attractive you are, how talented and smart you are, or how much money you have. It depends on how daring, persistent, and determined you are.

106 Do what you need to do today, and do not worry about tomorrow. Take things one day at a time.

107 Practice humility. Do not waste your time and energy bragging about your deeds and accomplishments.

108 Always be humble, but do not apologize for your success.

109 Do not be arrogant. Do not let your success go to your head and seduce you into thinking that you are invincible and can never lose.

110 Your level of success will be decided by your willingness to do whatever is necessary, within the laws and regulations, to get to your target, without any excuses.

111 Ignore distractions. Control your impulses to avoid doing what you are not supposed to do.

112 Sometimes luck is disguised as hard work. Do not miss the chance to create your own good luck.

113 The journey from point A to point B is determination, commitment, action, passion, and persistence.

114 No matter how great your goals are, you will never accomplish them unless you act and start working toward their realization.

115 If at first you do not accomplish what you want, try and try again until you succeed.

No matter what you do, do it to your utmost. I always attribute my success to always requiring myself to do my level best, if only in driving a tack in straight.

> Russel H. Conway

Every success is built on the ability to do better than just good enough.

> Unknown

Optimism is the faith that leads to achievement. Nothing can be done without hope or confidence.

> Helen Keller

Someone's opinion of you does not have to become your reality.

> Les Brown

Whether you think you can or whether you think you can't—you're right.

Henry Ford

Put all excuses aside and remember this: YOU are capable.

Zig Ziglar

5

SELF-DOUBT, FEAR and CRITICISM

116 Free yourself from self-doubt. Who are you not to create the life you want? Who are you not to achieve greatness? Who are you not to realize your dreams?

117 Never worry that your dreams are too big or your goals are too high. You may not achieve them all, but you will achieve far, far more than you have expected, and you will become a better and a more fulfilled person in the process.

118 Do not overestimate problems and do not underestimate your abilities.

119 When you face a new challenge, you have the opportunity to discover your own unique potential.

120 Be brave. Remember that bravery is not the lack of fear but the ability to move forward in spite of fear.

121 There are many things in life that we do not accomplish and many opportunities that we miss because of our fear to lose.

122 Sometimes it is very hard not to feel fear and sometimes our fears cause us to impose limitations on ourselves, but we can eliminate and conquer them by just continuing to move forward.

123 For some people, their fear to lose is greater than their desire to succeed, so they end up doing nothing and their dreams become impossible.

124 Make your desire to succeed stronger than your fear to lose.

125 Fear is good because it helps you to be cautious, but never let fear paralyzed you,

otherwise you will not be able to progress and accomplish what you want.

126 Yes, there is always some risk when you take action, but there is greater risk when you do not take any action.

127 Do not fear hard times because they often build character.

128 Do not fear making mistakes. Give yourself permission to make them, because making mistakes is what gives you experience and eventually that experience will help you minimize your mistakes.

129 Do not let yourself get overwhelmed or blinded by temporary setbacks to the point that you lose all hope and faith for a positive outcome.

130 Be willing to take educated risks, but do not gamble.

131 Every day, you get the opportunity to change your life. Change what you do not want. Change what makes you unhappy.

132 When you see an opportunity, act. Stop listening to people telling you why your idea will not work. Even though they may have good intentions, they may not know what they are talking about.

133 Everything that we do involves some kind of risk, but that is what makes life interesting and worthwhile.

134 Stay away from negative and pessimistic people.

135 Listen, but do not get too preoccupied with the opinions of others. In the end, your opinion is what counts.

136 Pay attention to criticism. Do not disregard it, but do not take it personally, do not let your ego get in the way, and do not let it affect your self-confidence. Keep on believing in yourself.

137 Criticism is just someone else's opinion. Even people who are experts in their fields are sometimes wrong. It is up to you to choose whether to believe some of it, none of it, or all of it. What *you* think is what counts.

138 Welcome criticism as constructive feedback; let it give you the opportunity to analyze your weaknesses and strengths so you can make the necessary improvements to realize your goals.

139 Self-criticism can be worse than the criticism from others. Never put yourself down. You may constructively criticize how and what you are doing to achieve your goals, but do not criticize yourself, because it is not healthy and will only get you down.

140 Erase self-doubt by working to build your strengths instead of focusing on your weaknesses.

141 Criticize only to help and advise—never do it to humiliate, insult, or degrade.

History will never accept difficulties as an excuse.

John F. Kennedy

We are what we pretend to be, so we must be careful about what we pretend to be.

Kurt Vonnegut

He who asks a question is a fool for a minute; he who does not remains a fool forever.

Chinese Proverb

The question is not what you look at, but what you see.

Henry David Thoreau

What lies behind us and what lies ahead of us are tiny matters compared to what lives within us.

>Ralph Waldo Emerson

6

POSITIVE THINKING and COMMUNICATION

142 Ask for help, advice, and guidance when needed.

143 Ask for what you want, ask for what you need, and if at first you do not succeed, keep asking.

144 Learn to listen—it is amazing how much we learn by doing so—it is relatively simple, right? So why don't more people do it?

145 Give yourself a break—give your ego a break. Do not stress yourself interrupting others while they are still talking—do not wait impatiently to finish their sentences. Practice, and in time you will become a better listener.

146 Listen to all people. There is something to learn from everybody, even those you perceive to be dull and ignorant.

147 Ask questions even if the answers seem obvious—you will be surprised that, many times, the answers are not as obvious as you thought.

148 Do not be embarrassed to say, "I don't know." It is amazing how much you can learn just by admitting that.

149 Do not allow your thoughts to control your actions. Be as strong as you can be, so you can force your actions to control your thoughts.

150 Remember that every creation starts with a thought.

151 Do not make yourself feel powerless. Do not make yourself feel like you are a "puppet" with no self-control whose strings are being pulled by someone else. Master your thoughts and actions.

152 Listen carefully to others. Try to understand them and then try to make yourself

understood. You will learn to communicate much better.

153 Make an effort to see things from the other person's point of view.

154 Always have honest and open communication with others.

155 Keep your mind open; let your thoughts wander and allow your brain and subconscious mind point you the direction to the answer you are seeking.

156 The quality of your life depends on the quality of your thoughts.

157 Change your way of thinking. If you think about what you do not want, you will only get more of it. Instead, think only about the things you want and the things you would like to bring into reality.

158 Always try to think positive. The brain can hold only one thought at a time—why not make that thought a positive one?

159 Practice thinking about only what you want in life. Little by little, you will notice that

what you do not want will begin to disappear.

160 Stop anticipating and expecting that things will go wrong, or else they will always will.

161 You will always get what you expect to get.

162 The only person that can stop you is yourself. Do not let that happen. Do not fill your subconscious mind with negative and self-defeating thoughts.

163 If you keep repeating long enough that you cannot do what you want to do, that you cannot become what you want to become, or that you cannot have the relationship that you want—your words will eventually evolve into a self-fulfilling prophecy.

164 You are what you think you are.

165 Do not empower your negative thoughts by giving them "legs" so they can run around your mind, creating worries, frustrations, and anxiety in your life.

166 Do not think and accept that you have no control over your life and future.

167 Stop thinking and assuming that what happens to you is your destiny. It is not. You will only be giving a message to your brain to stop looking for ideas or solutions. Thinking that way is only an excuse to relieve you from your responsibilities.

168 Pay attention to your thoughts and words, because they may come true.

169 Gain power over your negative thoughts before they rule your life. Maintain a positive and optimistic attitude believing that what you want can be achieved.

170 Do not make other people's negative thoughts yours. Learn to recognize them and do not make them part of your way of thinking.

171 Do not live by default. Learn to take control of your thoughts, your words, your feelings, and your actions. If you are in control of them, they can move you closer to your dreams, but if you are not careful, they can move you further away from them.

172 When you experience a negative circumstance or event, do not dwell on it.

Be proactive—put your attention on what you need to do to bring the situation to a positive result.

173 Remember, you always need the night in order to see and appreciate the stars.

Be not afraid of growing slowly; be afraid only of standing still.

Chinese Proverb

The real winners in life are the people who look at every situation with an expectation that they can make it work or make it better.

Barbara Pletcher

The only thing that stands between a man and what he wants from life is often merely the will to try it and the faith to believe that it is possible.

Richard M. DeVos

Good manners will open doors that the best education cannot.

Clarence Thomas

When one door of happiness closes, another opens; but often we look so long at the closed door that we do not see the one which has been opened for us.

Helen Keller

7

POSITIVE SELF-ESTEEM and GOOD MANNERS

174 Do not compare yourself with others. Celebrate the fact that you are unique—there is nobody else like you in the world, and you are capable of doing great and wonderful things with your life.

175 Always strive to be better than you used to be.

176 Learn to like yourself, learn to love yourself, not in a selfish or narcissistic way, but because you value your life and you are responsible for making it the best it can be.

177 You need to value yourself so you can value others, love yourself so you can love others,

respect yourself so you can respect others, and accept yourself so you can accept others. Keep in mind that nobody can give something he or she does not possess.

178 Learn to have a healthy respect for yourself.

179 Cultivate and maintain a positive self-esteem; it will motivate, energize, empower, and inspire you to achieve and reach your dreams, and you will become a better person in the process.

180 A positive self-esteem will help you face life's problems and opportunities in a more effective way. You will be more motivated by the desire to experience joy than by the desire to avoid pain.

181 See in yourself the person that you want to become—feel the joy of your achievements. See yourself as a success.

182 Be decisive. Do not be paralyzed with indecision—otherwise, you will miss opportunities and will not be able to move forward.

183 Do not overwhelm yourself with every single available piece of information. Trust your instincts and the knowledge that you already possess to make informed and educated decisions, but *decide.*

184 Always form a mental picture and feel the positive outcome of a particular situation or dilemma; play it and replay it, again and again.

185 Break away from the negative beliefs and ideas that have been passed on to you and that you have learned since you were born. You are responsible for yourself. You are capable of creating a better life for yourself.

186 Understand that you do not know or need to know everything. Understand your limitations, but do not let them be an excuse to stop learning and growing. Be curious and boost your knowledge.

187 We cannot know everything, but we can learn or get people who know to help us.

188 There will always be people who are more talented and people who are less talented than you are. The people who succeed,

though, are the ones with the courage to overcome challenges and are willing to press forward towards their success.

189 Believe in yourself and be a winner. Show confidence and respect—never show arrogance.

190 Work on the little things so you can have faith and trust in yourself to do the big things.

191 Do not focus on becoming the best—focus on doing *your* best and becoming the best will take care of itself.

192 If you apply yourself and do your best, you will find that you will never have any regrets.

193 Learn and accept that you cannot always please everybody; do not to get angry or frustrated. Of course, always do your best and be your best. Understand that some people are just hard to please, no matter what you do or how you do it.

194 Be assertive—speak your mind in an honest and direct way, but do not be insulting.

195 Learn to say no politely—you cannot be nor do everything for everybody. Remember, you have a life to live, too.

196 Never lose your good manners—do not become too serious or too self-important to say "please" and "thank you."

197 Always be considerate, polite and respectful.

198 Do not be shy—it does not help you. You will miss chances and opportunities in life.

199 Give a smile—it costs nothing. You will feel better and you can also make somebody's day.

200 Smile and introduce yourself when entering a gathering full of strangers.

In every man there is something wherein I may learn of him, and in that I am his pupil.

Ralph Waldo Emerson

I had six honest serving men. They taught me all I knew. Their names were: Where, What, When, Why, How, and Who.

Rudyard Kipling

Research shows that you begin learning in the womb and go right on learning until the moment you pass on. Your brain has a capacity for learning that is virtually limitless, which makes every human a potential genius.

Michael J. Gelb

Learning is not attained by chance; it must be sought for with ardor and diligence.

Abigail Adams

All of the top achievers I know are life-long learners ... looking for new skills, insights, and ideas. If they're not learning, they're not growing ... not moving toward excellence.

Denis Waitley

8
LEARNING and UNDERSTANDING

201 Surround yourself with great people. Look for them, be around them, talk to them, read about them, and learn from them. Most great people like to share their advice and wisdom.

202 Read as much as you can, expand your mind; you will not only exercise your brain, but you will increase your knowledge, you will learn from the experiences of others, you will travel to new places, you will discover new cultures and you will expand the way you see and do things.

203 Study, learn, observe, listen, practice, and do. Become a more knowledgeable, able, and informed person. Create choices for yourself, so you can have the freedom to choose your own destiny—otherwise you may find that someone else will do the choosing for you, and you may not like the choices you are given.

204 Have an open mind; be open to changes, alternatives, or ideas that may lead you to accomplish what you want or desire.

205 Be open to trying new things so you can learn new things.

206 Do not be fooled by "great" first impressions. Sometimes, appearances can be deceiving.

207 Do not be too quick to judge a book by its cover. You may be delighted by what you find inside.

208 When you learn something new, it may be hard, uncomfortable, or awkward in the beginning. But anything becomes easier through practice and constant repetition; the more you do something, the easier it becomes.

209 Practice until what you practice becomes a habit. Keep on doing it until it just flows naturally and becomes part of you. Do it until you feel very comfortable, until you can do it without thinking.

210 Teach what you have learned. It is the best way to practice what you already know.

211 Do not stop learning. Be an effective learner. Commit to bettering yourself professionally, personally, and spiritually.

212 We live in a wonderful world now where information is abundant and readily available. Take advantage of it.

213 Knowledge is not power, but the use and application of knowledge is.

214 Keep yourself informed, but do not let your mind become inundated with negative news and reports.

215 Write down affirmations of what you want to create, change, or achieve, and read them daily. This will help you manage and guide your thoughts and ideas.

216 Be wise. Do not let your ego get in the way of things, and do not let your pride get in the way of your life.

217 Avoid impulses. Learn to control your emotions.

218 Change your moods through positive action.

219 Learn to control your moods before they control you. Understand that, like the seasons, your moods will change all the time.

220 Do not take things personally. Try to recognize and understand the moods of others—some people do not know how to control their thoughts, feelings, and emotions.

221 Everybody has ups and downs. Somebody may not be nice today but could be a pleasure to approach tomorrow—recognize this fact and use it to your advantage.

222 Acknowledge your bad habits and get rid of them by replacing them with good habits.

223 They say that we use only 10 percent of our full mental potential. Strive to develop and use the other 90 percent.

224 Learn to delegate tasks and chores.

225 Be smart by hiring people that are smarter than you are.

226 Do not pretend to know everything. Hire somebody who knows how to get things done right the first time.

227 If you have to pay more for a job well done, do it! It will be worth it. You will get what you pay for and you will save yourself headaches later on.

He is rich or poor according to what he is, not according to what he has.

Henry Ward Beecher

If a person gets his attitude toward money straight, it will help straighten out almost every other area in his life.

Billy Graham

If money be not thy servant, it will be thy master. The covetous man cannot so properly be said to possess wealth, as that may be said to possess him.

Francis Bacon

If money is your hope for independence you will never have it. The only real security that a man will have in this world is a reserve of knowledge, experience, and ability.

Henry Ford

A man should always consider how much he has more than he wants, and how much more unhappy he might be than he really is.

Joseph Addison

9
MONEY

228 Organize your financial records. Watch your expenses, especially the little ones. You may not even think about them, but they add up. Combined, they will become big expenses that you may fail to notice.

229 Always spend less than you earn. Change your habits and your attitude about money—your financial wealth will depend on how well you manage it.

230 Invest for your future—plan, set financial goals and establish a financial foundation. Unfortunately, many people retire with nothing, not because they plan to fail, but because they fail to plan.

231 Some people spend more time planning their next vacation than planning their lives. Do not make that mistake.

232 Do your homework. Have a clear financial goal. Building wealth is not a matter of luck— it is a matter of choice.

233 Remember—it is not how much money you make, but how much money you get to keep.

234 Set up an automatic saving and/or investment plan. Check with your bank or financial institution. Set some money aside for savings or investments first, before you pay for everything else. Do it for the long term. In no time, you will realize that you have more money than you originally thought.

235 Organize and manage your financial records. Keep your expenses in check. If you have debt, create a debt-reduction plan.

236 Pay off your house as soon as you can—it will bring you great satisfaction and peace of mind not to have house payments anymore.

237 Invest in real estate and invest for the long term. It is one of the best investments against inflation.

238 When you use credit cards, do so only for convenience. Pay the balance in full every month.

239 Do not live on credit. Do not spend money that you do not have on things that you do not really need.

240 Do not think that something that has a designer label and costs more is better made and of better quality. Quite often, what you are buying is just the name.

241 Learn how to spend your money. Some people overspend, while some do not spend enough, even when they have plenty of it. Always be responsible about your financial obligations. Manage them well, save, invest, share, and pay your debts, but also enjoy your money and what your money gives you.

242 Keep money circulating. You will not be able to take it with you once you are gone from this world.

243 Understand the law of return. Whatever money you give unselfishly will return to you many times over.

244 It is wonderful to have money. It is wonderful to get all the things that money can buy, but it is also wonderful to keep and maintain the things that money cannot buy. No matter what, make sure you never lose those!

245 Many people are so poor that the only thing they have is money. Cultivate your spiritual growth.

246 Teach your kids the value of money. Teach them from an early age the importance of managing, saving, and investing.

Never let the future disturb you. You will meet it, if you have to, with the same weapons of reason which today arm you against the present.

Marcus Aurelius

Do you remember the things you were worrying about a year ago? How did they work out? Didn't you waste a lot of fruitless energy on account of most of them? Didn't most of them turn out all right after all?

Dale Carnegie

If you cannot help worrying, remember that worrying cannot help you, either.

Unknown

If you employed study, thinking, and planning time daily, you could develop and use the power that can change the course of your destiny.

W. Clement Stone

Before you speak, listen. Before you write, think. Before you spend, earn. Before you invest, investigate. Before you criticize, wait. Before you pray, forgive. Before you quit, try. Before you retire, save. Before you die, give.

William A. Ward

10
PLANNING, PAST, PRESENT and FUTURE

247 Learn to plan, organize and manage your time efficiently. We all have twenty-four hours a day, seven days a week whether we are the president of United States, a CEO of a corporation, a doctor, or a janitor.

248 How you plan your day and set your priorities is what makes a difference between what you can and cannot accomplish.

249 Many people seem to be busy all the time running here and there, but they never seem to accomplish anything because they do not have a plan.

250 Value your time and effort. Do not be lazy. It is funny that some people don't have time to do things right the first time, but they always seem to have time to do them over again a second time.

251 Live in the present. Consider the past only to remind you not to repeat the same mistakes again. Consider the future only to make appropriate and necessary plans for your success.

252 Do not waste your time thinking about your past problems, setbacks, disappointments, heartaches, or disillusions.

253 Do not cling to the past. Otherwise, you will not be able to live your present with the utmost satisfaction and joy.

254 You can never go back to where you were before. You can only start now with all of your passion to create a different and better reality for yourself.

255 Yesterday is gone and you cannot do anything to bring it back. Leave it behind. Do not spoil today tormenting yourself about yesterday.

256 Worrying uses your imagination in a negative way and creates an emotional burden that robs you from living life to the fullest.

257 Do not be too concerned about tomorrow. Have faith and do what you need and have to do, to the best of your ability, to create your future, but do not waste today worrying about what might happen.

258 Do not live your life imagining and creating tragedies in your mind that will probably never take place.

259 Avoid upsetting and tormenting yourself over events that you will never see.

260 Stop stressing yourself about things over which you have no control, because there is nothing you can do about them. If there are things you have control over, there is no need to worry about them.

261 Understand that worrying will not help you with the problems of tomorrow but can ruin the happiness of today.

262 Do not get so busy making a living that you forget to create a life.

263 Learn to balance your life and avoid extremes. Always make time for your work, time for your family, time for your friends, and time for yourself.

264 If you separate the time devoted to work from the time devoted to yourself and your family, you will have a more rewarding life.

265 Do not take for granted your family and friends. They are the greatest riches you have. Always take care of them.

266 Do not wait for something bad to happen before you realize what is important in your life. Keep your priorities straight.

The human race has one really effective weapon, and that is laughter.

Mark Twain

Laugh at yourself and at life. Not in the spirit of derision or whining self-pity, but as a remedy, a miracle drug, that will ease your pain, cure your depression, and help you to put in perspective that seemingly terrible defeat and worry, thus freeing your mind to think clearly toward the solution that is certain to come. Never take yourself too seriously.

Og Mandino

Laughter is the shortest distance between two people.

Victor Borge

Laughter can be more satisfying than honor; more precious than money; more heart-cleansing than prayer.

Harriet Rochlin

11
LAUGHING and TAKING it EASY

267 Take time, slow down, and contemplate the world around you. Enjoy and savor every moment.

268 Sometimes what we think is the most insignificant daily routine could turn into the most wonderful source of joy.

269 Learn to relax and do nothing, it will help you clear your mind and rest your body.

270 Do not overreact—do not blow things out of proportion—do not become angry and uptight if things do not turn out the way you expected.

271 Allow yourself to laugh. Laugh at yourself and laugh at the world. Take it easy. Follow the advice from Bobby Mc Ferrin's song and … "Don't worry, be happy".

272 Laugh often, because that is the way to relax and massage your body and soul.

273 The best remedy to cure your stress is laughter.

274 A good sense of humor and laughter will help you maintain a more optimistic and positive outlook in times of adverse and difficult situations.

275 Laugh, relax, recharge your body, and regain your energy.

276 Laugh at today. Everything that is happening today will seem insignificant later on with the passing of time.

277 Laughter is the best medicine. It is good for your body, it is good for your mind, and it is good for your soul.

278 Always laugh to put yourself in a better mood and to reduce the stress that you may be feeling.

279 Laughter is contagious; share the benefits with others around you.

280 Have a good sense of humor and laugh. It will help you relieve tension and it will help you in your interactions with others.

281 Laugh even if you do not feel like it. You will notice that little by little your mood will begin to change and you will feel relieved.

282 Find humor in everyday life; avoid taking life too seriously.

283 Understand that everything that you are enduring or feeling right now—even the great moments—will pass. Be grateful for the experience, learn the lessons, and move on.

284 Take your goals and plans seriously, but not so seriously to the point that you neglect yourself, your family, and the people around you.

285 Take it easy. Be at peace with yourself. Keep in mind that every experience in your life will be replaced by another experience.

You should never marry someone hoping to change them; you should marry someone hoping they will never change.

Colby Bates

Present your family and friends with their eulogies now—they won't be able to hear how much you love them and appreciate them from inside the coffin.

Unknown

The quality of your life is the quality of your relationships.

Anthony Robbins

The problem with relationships is that people are so busy falling in love that they forget to fall in like.

Unknown

My marriage brought me neither happiness nor pain. My husband and I hardly spoke to each other. This wasn't because we were angry. We had nothing to say.

Marilyn Monroe

12

LOVE and RELATIONSHIPS

286 Learn to enjoy and appreciate every single beautiful detail that life and your loved ones offer you.

287 Love with all your passion and without any reservation. Even though you may get hurt, you will live your life to the fullest.

288 Keep in mind that a great love, like any success in life, involves some kind of risk. Go ahead—*take it!*

289 Do not let your ego or personal pride get in the way of your relationship. In the end, it doesn't matter who is right but what is right.

290 In a relationship, do not take the other person for granted. Let your mate be who he or she really is—do not try to change or control him or her.

291 Do no put conditions on the love that you give. Accept people the way they are. Do not expect and demand that people fit your mold before you love them.

292 In relationships, opposites do attract but not in the long run.

293 To keep a healthy and successful relationship, you have to watch it, work at it, nurture it, pay attention to it, and care for it. You must do all this on a consistent basis.

294 Love is a great part of a relationship, but it is not all.

295 Always tell your loved ones what they mean to you and how much you appreciate them.

296 Do not enter into a relationship expecting to get something. Instead, enter into a relationship willing to give something.

297 You do not have to be compatible with your mate in everything, but you have to be compatible in most things.

298 In a relationship, if you have to express your point of view, do it! Debate, argue, express your opinion, but never insult.

299 Do not become possessive. The purpose of a relationship is to complement each other, grow together, and achieve your common goals as a couple. At the same time, you must each maintain your individual identity as a human being.

300 Do not become controlling, or you will not be able to control the relationship.

301 Do not be jealous. You will poison your soul by letting your imagination wander. Do not allow your mind to create incredible stories without any foundation.

302 Relationships can be hard sometimes, but instead of trying to find reasons not to be together, look for and find reasons to be together.

303 When in a relationship, do not waste your mental energy expecting your chores and responsibilities to be shared equally, sometimes you have to do and give 100 percent and it is fine. Just do things as they need to be done, regardless of whose turn it is.

304 Practice communication and understanding to achieve a healthy relationship with your significant other.

305 Do not get too comfortable with silence; if there is a problem, talk it over. The issue, problem, or situation is not going to go away by itself. If you do not talk about it, it may only get worse.

306 Honesty, sincerity, respect, integrity, and reliability are ingredients that build trust and hold relationship together.

307 Surprise your loved one with flowers—just because … it is a great way to say "I am thinking of *you*."

308 It is not a matter of just finding the right partner, but also of being the right one.

309 Try to find yourself first. Take a look inside of yourself before you try to find your significant other.

310 Love yourself, mature, and evolve so you can be prepared to love someone else and have a healthy relationship.

311 You do not have to find a partner that is perfect—you just have to find the one that is perfect for you.

312 Do not spend more time planning your wedding than you spend planning your marriage.

313 Marry for love. Do not marry just to get a better future, because eventually, you will wish that you could get back to your past.

314 To make your relationship a fulfilling one, make your love, communication, and understanding greater than the need that you feel for one another.

315 Always look for someone who makes your heart smile, no matter what.

316 Do not waste your time trying to find a perfect person; instead, learn to see an imperfect person perfectly.

317 Value and appreciate the closeness of your spouse, your children, and your family.

318 Strive to create a life of harmony at home.

We cannot always build the future of our youth, but we can build our youth for the future.

Franklin Delano Roosevelt

You may give them your love but not your thoughts. For they have their own thoughts. You may house their bodies but not their souls, for their souls dwell in the house of tomorrow, which you cannot visit, not even in your dreams.

Kahlil Gibran

Ask the young, they know everything.

Joubert

Discipline is a symbol of caring to a child. He needs guidance. If there is love, there is no such thing as being too tough with a child. A parent must also not be afraid to hang himself. If you have never been hated by your child, you have never been a parent.

Bette Davis

13

CHILDREN

319 Tell your spouse and children how much you love them every day. Do not just assume that they already know.

320 Do not try to be your children's "friend." I am sure your children have plenty of friends of their own.

321 Be a parent and act like one! That is what your children need. Do not spoil them. Give them all your love, but instill discipline and respect.

322 Be involved in your children's life. Listen to them, talk to them, get to know their friends, and get to know their interests.

323 Give your kids your time, attention, love, and affection. Do not try to use material things as a substitute for your time, attention, love, and affection.

324 Do not try to live your life through your children's lives. Do not be selfish. Let them be whatever they want to be, let them have and dream their own dreams.

325 Instill in your children the habit of reading at an early age. This habit will help them exercise and expand their minds.

326 Help your children develop a solid moral view by teaching and explaining to them good character traits such as honesty, loyalty, compassion, and respect for others.

327 Minimize the time your children spend watching television, playing video games, and "surfing" the Internet.

328 Let your children have their own thoughts— do not try to make them like you.

We are all full of weakness and errors; let us mutually pardon each other our follies

>Voltaire

Consider how much more you often suffer from your anger and grief, than from those very things for which you are angry and grieved.

>Marcus Antonius

Forgive all who have offended you, not for them, but for yourself.

>Harriet Nelson

A wise man will make haste to forgive, because he knows the full value of time and will not suffer it to pass away in unnecessary pain.
>Rambler

Forgiveness ... is a willingness to get over what you think should have happened and an acceptance of the reality of what actually happened.

Rhonda Britten

14

FORGIVENESS and ACCEPTANCE

329 Believe in the power of forgiveness. Do not let it stand in the way of your happiness. It will set you free.

330 Do not hold resentments or grudges—they are a waste of your mental energy.

331 Close the door of your past and continue moving forward to a better future.

332 The stronger you are, the more able you will be to forgive.

333 Let other people have the last word.

334 If you feel like you want to forgive, do it! The past will not be changed, but your future will be illuminated.

335 Learn to love someone when they least deserve it, because that is when they need your love most.

336 Do not believe that being right is more important than being happy.

337 Do not pass judgment before you learn the two sides of the story.

338 Do not just assume anything—when in doubt, ask. Otherwise, your assumption could be wrong and could lead to problems and misunderstandings.

339 Do not harbor any prejudice against color, religion, creed, politics, culture, or gender preference. We are all created equal; we are all a part of the human race.

340 Do not worry about what people think of you.

341 Everybody is unique. Respect the fact that we are all different; we all have different

preferences, different ideas, and different points of view.

342 Be tolerant. Live and let live. Refrain from judgment—allow people to be, dress, and act differently.

343 Do not expect everybody to fit your mold of perfection. You will only get frustrated and disappoint yourself.

344 Be more relaxed with your imperfections—you will then be more tolerant of the imperfections of others.

345 Do not envy others because they have achieved greatness and success in life. You can be living that life, too, if you study them and learn from them.

True happiness is to enjoy the present, without anxious dependence upon the future, not to amuse ourselves with either hopes or fears but to rest satisfied with what we have, which is sufficient, for he that is so wants nothing. The great blessings of mankind are within us and within our reach. A wise man is content with his lot, whatever it may be, without wishing for what he has not.

Seneca

Remember that very little is needed to make a happy life; it is all within yourself, in your way of thinking.

Marcus Aurelius

We act as though comfort and luxury were the chief requirements of life, when all that we need to make us really happy is something to be enthusiastic about.

Charles Kingsley

Health is the greatest possession. Contentment is the greatest treasure. Confidence is the greatest friend. Non-being is the greatest joy.

Lao Tzu

15

HAPPINESS and AWARENESS

346 Take the time to take care of yourself, take time to take care of your body. If you do not, eventually you will have to find the time to be sick.

347 Maintain balanced and healthy eating habits, incorporating into your diet fruits, vegetables, and whole grains.

348 Eat to live—do not live to eat.

349 Keep your body hydrated by drinking at least eight glasses of water every day.

350 If you consume alcoholic drinks, do so in moderation.

351 Do not smoke. Do not use drugs.

352 Take care of your body and your body will take care of you.

353 Create the habit of exercising and meditating at least three times a week.

354 Sleep well every night by keeping a regular schedule. It will help with your mood and your concentration.

355 Do not fool yourself into believing that all of the high-tech gadgets and devices we have now are freeing more of your time. They will not necessarily make your life better or easier.

356 Do not try to do everything at the same time. Relax! All of the gadgets and appliances we have are supposed to make our lives easier, more comfortable, and relaxed, yet we are more stressed than ever—find balance.

357 Let the cell phone rest and give yourself a break, too. You do not have to answer every single call that you receive.

358 Do not clutter your life with things you do not need or use. Get rid of them, and be open to receiving new and better things in your life.

359 Travel as much as you can—there is a big world out there. You will meet interesting people, learn from different cultures, and become wiser in the process.

360 The grass is not always greener on the other side.

361 Enjoy the happiness that you have today and make the best out of every day. Get busy working on your goals and dreams, that way, you will avoid being sad.

362 Find your vocation, find your career—do what you like, and love with all your passion—your life will be wonderful, and your rewards will be plenty.

363 Do not become too obsessed trying to achieve what you do not yet possess,

without paying attention to what you already have.

364 Your happiness and peace of mind will not come from getting what you want, but from learning to love and appreciate what you already have.

365 Stop complaining. Chances are you already have everything you need to lead a wonderful life. Unfortunately, many times, this fact is very hard to comprehend, because we think that getting more and achieving more will make us happy.

366 Think more about what you already have instead of what you want, and little by little, you will start realizing that what you have is not so bad after all. Eventually, you will see your life with a different point of view, and you will see that it is much better than you thought.

367 The way you choose your life will create your happiness.

368 Do not make the mistake of thinking that more is better; otherwise, you will never be satisfied.

369 Do not think and assume that more money is going to make you happy.

370 Do not think and assume that acquiring new and more things is going to make you happy.

371 Do not think and assume that achieving more goals is going to make you happy.

372 Do not think and assume that a new relationship is going to make you happy.

373 Your life is driven from within. Peace and happiness are inside of you—search your soul and your heart. Be at peace with yourself and let happiness come out from inside of you.

374 Take responsibility for your own happiness— do not expect people or things to bring you happiness, or you could be disappointed.

375 Thinking that something external from you will bring you peace, fulfillment, equilibrium, love, and happiness is a fantasy that will only bring you frustration.

376 You are as happy as you think you are.

377 Happiness is an attitude, not a destination.

378 Be friendly and spend time with people, especially the ones you love. This is an ingredient for a happier life.

379 We all experience hard times at one point or another in our lives, but no matter what happens, remember that misery is optional—you do not really have to participate in it.

380 Do not forget that after every storm, the sun always shines again.

381 Do not put your happiness on hold until you are done with everything you want to do, because you will never be done. There will always be something to do. Do what you need to do but take the time to "stop and smell the roses."

382 Always be good to others—always be willing to help others. Your level of happiness will increase and your heart will be healthier with joy.

383 Have a purpose and build the passion to squeeze every single minute and make every single day a wonderful day.

384 Erase from your vocabulary the word "someday." Do not save things for "special occasions." Take into account the fact that every day is special. Every day is a gift that we must appreciate and be thankful for. Wear your attractive clothes, wear your nice perfume, use your fine silverware and dishes, and drink from your expensive crystal glasses ... just because. Live every day to the fullest and savor every minute of it.

385 Help other people. Donate your time and money often, not only when asked.

386 Be compassionate. Recognize the pain, problems, and frustrations that other people may be feeling.

387 Open your heart and help others less fortunate. Help others so they can help themselves.

388 When you do a favor, do not expect or ask for one in return.

389 You cannot recycle time or save it in a drawer for later use. Do not postpone your life.

390 Always concentrate on the path that you have planned for yourself. Strive to be the best that you can be. Dare to be great!

Let us rise up and be thankful, for if we didn't learn a lot today, at least we learned a little, and if we didn't learn a little, at least we didn't get sick, and if we got sick, at least we didn't die; so, let us all be thankful.

Buddha

A thankful heart is not only the greatest virtue, but the parent of all the other virtues.

Cicero

Thank you, dear God For all You have given me, for all You have taken away from me, for all You have left me.

Unknown

If a fellow isn't thankful for what he's got, he isn't likely to be thankful for what he's going to get.

Frank A. Clark

In our daily lives, we must see that it is not happiness that makes us grateful, but the gratefulness that makes us happy.

Albert Clarke

16

GRATITUDE and GETTING OLDER

391 Take a moment every day and be thankful for what you have.

392 Acknowledge and express your gratitude to all the people who help you achieve your goals. Give many thanks to all the people who help you become the person that you want to become. Thank all of those who have helped you get where you wanted to go.

393 Pay your bills with gratitude and be thankful that you have the money to spend.

394 Being thankful helps you understand and appreciate that what you already have is really more than enough.

395 Show gratitude. We all have reasons to be grateful. Keep in mind, recognize, and write down all the things that you are grateful for—your family, your friends, your health, your work.

396 Show your appreciation and constantly give thanks to everyone who means something in your life.

397 Never grow old. Age is just a number to keep track of how long you have been here. As long as your heart is young, you will never grow old.

398 Never stop playing. Never stop learning— if you continue to play and learn you will never be old.

399 Do not fear the effects of time, because time cannot destroy the creative powers of your mind and body.

400 Your age is an asset. Feel great about your wisdom, your talent, your skills, and the

experience that you gathered throughout your life.

401 Retire from your job or your vocation if want or must, but never retire from life.

402 As you grow older, do not view your physical limitations as a burden. Instead, see them as an opportunity to focus on other activities that can reward you with pleasure and satisfaction.

403 You are not growing old—you are only growing more experienced.

404 Continue to stimulate your brain with mental activities, and maintain your creativity and curiosity. Continue learning and making spiritual progress and you will keep your vitality as you grow older.

405 Above all, live your life with a purpose—looking forward to something every morning.

406 No matter how old you are, never stop dreaming.

407 You may have a wrinkled face as you grow older, and that is fine, but if you lose your enthusiasm for life, you will end up with a wrinkled soul.

408 Reject all the stereotypes about old age and embrace life. Envision yourself healthy, vigorous, happy, radiant, and powerful.

409 May you have a wonderful, happy, peaceful, prosperous, and rewarding life. Enjoy it to the fullest! Bear in mind, in the end, the only things that you will regret are the chances you never took, the time you did not spend with your family and friends, the places you did not see, and the things you did not do.

Your time is limited, so don't waste it living someone else's life. Don't be trapped by dogma– which is living with the results of other people's thinking. Don't let the noise of other's opinions drown out your own inner voice, and most important, have the courage to follow your heart and intuition. They somehow already know what you truly want to become. Everything else is secondary.

Steve Jobs

And in the end, it's not the years in your life that count. It's the life in your years.

Abraham Lincoln

FINAL THOUGHTS

I hope and wish the *Advice My Parents Gave Me and Other Lessons I Learned from My Mistakes* helps you, inspires and motivates you to start and/or continue in your journey to become a better person and achieve the success you desire.

In the end, you will never regret the things you have done, but you will regret the things that you have not done. With that in mind, dare yourself to take more chances, dare yourself to make mistakes and learn from them, dare yourself to take more trips, dare yourself to smile more often and say I love you more often, dare yourself to spend more time with your family and friends, dare yourself to give a helping hand, dare yourself to stop for a moment and "smell the roses," dare yourself not to worry and stress too much, dare yourself to be successful—dare yourself to be happy.

At the same time, learn not to fear a negative outcome; it may be the opportunity for a better and more educated start next time. Do not fear the unknown; otherwise, you will never be able to move forward. Do not fear commitment; decide, set goals, make plans, and strive to achieve the success you dream. Do not fear disapproval or rejection; you cannot always please everybody, not everybody will like you, not everybody will like your ideas, not everybody will think like you, but you know what? That is OK. Most of all, do not fear success; you have the power, within you, to be a better person and have a better life.

Become the person that you want to be; be a winner. You do not have to keep on doing things the way you have always done them. Take charge of your life, because your life depends on you. Face your challenges one by one; stop finding excuses to satisfy your ego; give your word to yourself and carry through on it. Be honest with yourself—acknowledge that there are good things about you, that you know good things and have good traits, but, like everyone one of us, you need to learn and/or improve some things. Always respect and learn from those who know more than you do. Do more than you have to do—go the extra mile.

Today is the time to change your old life for a better one. What are you waiting for? Start *now*! Live your life to the fullest—enjoy and take advantage of every single moment. May all your wishes and dreams come true. Today is the first day of the rest of your life. Do something about it! May you live a wonderful, peaceful, happy, prosperous, and successful life.

Rodolfo Costa

ABOUT THE AUTHOR

Rodolfo Costa was born in Lima, Peru. At age nineteen, without knowing what to expect, he said goodbye to his parents and immigrated to the United States. Through the difficulties and joys of life, with the advice received and the mistakes made, he learned to embrace the world in a different and more positive way, and now with immense gratitude for the knowledge he gained, he is able to share his earned wisdom in his new inspirational and motivational collection *Advice My Parents Gave Me and Other Lessons I Learned From My Mistakes.* Today, Rodolfo Costa continues his learning, sharing his knowledge, and evolving as a person and human being. He is a business owner, a Realtor, a teacher, and always a student. He lives in Northern California.

Made in the USA
Charleston, SC
11 January 2012